DONNA BRYANT is a native New Zealander who
specializes in writing books and television scripts for children.
Her previous books include the 'One Day' series
(*One Day in the Garden* and other titles), the 'Play School' series
and the 'Wildtracker' series, all published by Hodder & Stoughton.
Donna has always shared her home with animals.
At the moment she has two cats, Bamford and Buster,
and a 'mad' Rhode Island Red hen.

JAKKI WOOD studied graphic design at Wolverhampton
Polytechnic. She is a very successful children's book illustrator,
whose previous books include *There's A Monster Under my Bed*
and *One Bear with Bees in his Hair* (ABC), and
Happy Christmas, Ginger (Collins), which she also wrote.
Jakki Wood lives and works in London.

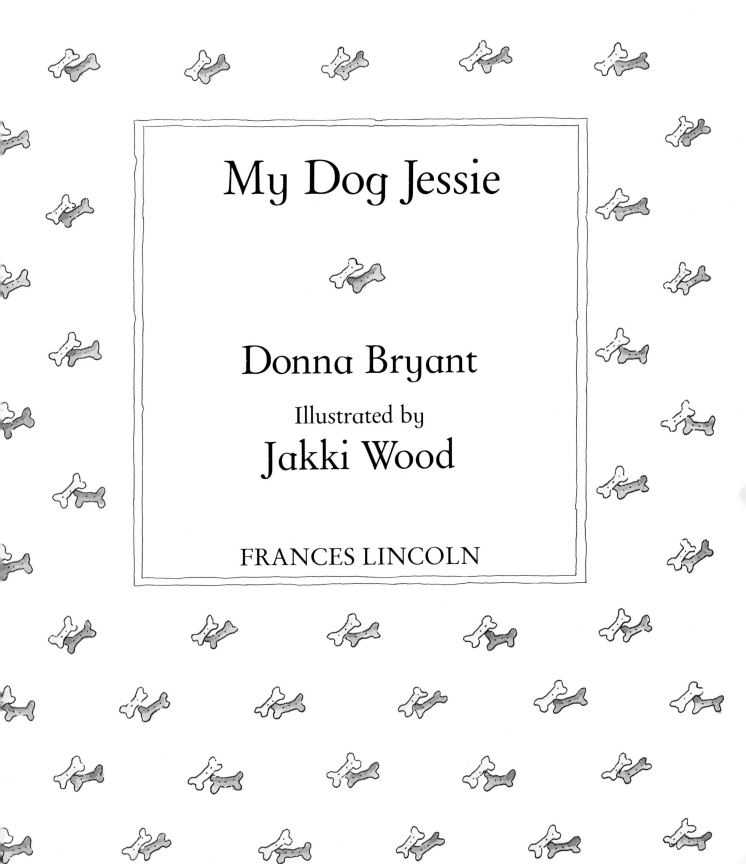

My Dog Jessie

Donna Bryant

Illustrated by
Jakki Wood

FRANCES LINCOLN

My dog Jessie used to be a puppy.

Now she is nearly as big as me!

Every day we play together,

and go for a walk.

Jessie likes to chase cats!

She also likes riding in the car . . .

swimming . . .

and drying herself afterwards!

Jessie loves to sleep in her basket.

When I scratch her tummy she wags
her tail.

Jessie is always hungry.

I'm glad she likes brussel sprouts.

She loves something to chew,

and she buries bones where no one
will find them.

Jessie knows all the dogs in our
neighbourhood.

She barks at strangers.

But when she sees me . . .

Jessie smiles!

For Sushi and Jessie D.B.
For Rebecca Neal J.W.

Text copyright © Donna Bryant 1991
Illustrations copyright © Jakki Wood 1991

First published in Great Britain in 1991 by
Frances Lincoln Limited, Apollo Works
5 Charlton Kings Road, London NW5 2SB

British Library Cataloguing in Publication Data
Bryant, Donna
My dog Jessie.
1. Dogs
I. Title   II. Wood, Jacqueline *1957–*
636.7

ISBN 0-7112-0655-4   hardback
ISBN 0-7112-0656-2   paperback

Printed and bound in Hong Kong

First Frances Lincoln Edition: May 1991

1   3   5   7   9   8   6   4   2